The **Sophia Day**™ Creative Team-
Kayla Pearson, Timothy Zowada,
Stephanie Strouse, Megan Johnson, Mel Sauder

Designed by Stephanie Strouse

Published and Distributed by MVP Kids Media, LLC
Mesa, Arizona, USA
Printed by RR Donnelley Asia Printing Solutions, Ltd
Dongguan City, Guangdong Province, China
DOM Jan 2018, Job # 03-001-01

help**me**
BECOME™

Overcoming *Selfishness* &
Becoming *Considerate*™

REAL
mvpkids®

Stomp Out Selfishness™

SHORT STORIES

Written by Kayla Pearson   *Illustrated by* Timothy Zowada

TABLE OF CONTENTS

Yong's Saturday Morning Show

HIYAH!

Yong drove a punch through the air.
He looked forward to watching
the Amazing Buddy Hero
on Saturday mornings.

The Amazing Buddy Hero was so *fast* and **STRONG**. He always stopped the villains. Some kids at Yong's school were like those villains. They were mean to Yong. He wished he could be like the Amazing Buddy Hero.

Yong raced into the living room. His older sister, Lilly, was already watching TV. He *grabbed* the remote and said,

"It's my turn!"

"Hey! Change it back! My show isn't done yet!" Yong and Lilly wrestled over the remote.

6

"What's going on in here?"
Gong-Gong, their grandfather,
came into the room.

"I was watching my show and Yong
changed it! He's being so *selfish*!"
Lilly glared at Yong.

"It's *my* turn to watch
Amazing Buddy Hero!"

"Yong, give the remote back to your sister and come in here with me."
Yong threw the remote back at his sister and

stomped over

to his grandfather.

"What's wrong?" Gong-Gong asked.
"This is not like you."

"*Nothing*, I just really want to watch my show."

"Tell me something. *Who do you want to be like*, the Amazing Buddy Hero or the villains?"

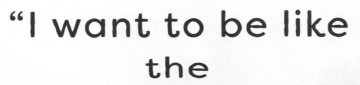

"I want to be like
the
AMAZING
BUDDY
HERO,"

Yong replied.

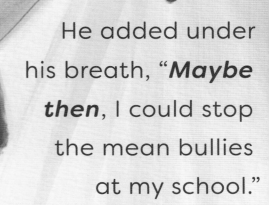

He added under
his breath, "**Maybe
then**, I could stop
the mean bullies
at my school."

"I see. Do you think that the Amazing Buddy Hero would steal the remote from his sister? *Or is that something the villains would do?*"

"Something the villains would do," muttered Yong.

"That's right. Your sister was watching first, so you need to wait. She wasn't doing anything wrong when you came in and took over. **That's what bullies do.**"

Yong hung his head down.
Gong-Gong was right.

"I'm sorry for not being considerate," Yong apologized to Lilly. "You were there first and I wouldn't like it if you did that to me."

Lilly smiled back and said,
"I forgive you, little brother."

"Well then, how about you take me outside and show me your blocks and kicks, Yong," Gong-Gong suggested.

"Will you teach me some Kung Fu?" Yong asked with excitement.

"Yes, I think you're ready to learn, as long as you remember to **put others first** and not become a bully yourself."

18

THINK & TALK ABOUT IT

YONG'S SATURDAY MORNING SHOW

Discuss the story...

1. What did Yong do that was selfish?

2. Why did Yong act selfishly?

3. What should Yong have done instead?

4. How did Yong make it right with Lilly?

5. What did Gong-Gong teach Yong about being considerate?

Discuss how to apply the story...

1. Is there something you and your sibling or friend have a hard time sharing?

2. What is something you could do next time instead?

3. Have you ever forgiven someone for being selfish toward you?

4. Has someone ever forgiven you? How did it feel when they forgave you?

5. Think of a villain you know. How do they act selfishly?

6. What are some examples of different ways you could be like a hero?

FOR PARENTS & MENTORS: *Help your child overcome selfishness by talking about admirable heroes. Look at the good things they do and talk about how your child can be like them. At the same time, you can look at what bad things the villains do and talk about how we do not want to imitate those behaviors. Be sure to monitor the media your child watches to eliminate negative influences.*

Olivia's Special Sister Time

"How many more minutes until Lucy gets here?"

Olivia asked her parents as she looked out the window.
She was excited to spend time with her big sister.
Her parents were leaving for a couple of hours while
they had special sister time.

"Looks like she is walking up now," said Olivia's mom.

Olivia RUSHED to the door.

She gave Lucy a **BIG** hug
when she walked in the house.

"I brought a special craft for us to do today! Who wants to do it with me?" Lucy asked her sisters.

"I do! I do!"

Olivia and Marie answered jumping up and down.

"I just want to read my book," said Darcy, Olivia's older sister.

They said "goodbye" to their parents and began to set up the craft.

"Today we're going to make balloon bowls.
It might be a little tricky.
We all need to _work together._"

step 1

"Fill up the balloon with air."

"I'LL DO THAT! I just learned how to blow up a balloon last week. Let me show you!" Olivia grabbed the balloon, filled it with air and tied it.

"WOW! That's pretty impressive, Olivia!" Lucy exclaimed.

28

step 2

"Paint glue onto the bottom half of the balloon."

"**Oh! Oh!**
Give ME the brush!
I can do that!"
said Olivia.

"I think it is Marie's
turn to help," said Lucy
handing the brush
to Marie.

"But I want to do it!
Marie has a hard time
with that kind of stuff.
She will just mess it up.
Let ME do it!"

"Olivia, I know you are excited, but we all need to work together. We cannot just think about ourselves. Marie wants to help just as much as you do. **We should think about** putting others first."

Olivia pouted. She really wanted to be the one to do it, but she watched as Marie painted the glue on the balloon.

Marie had a hard time controlling the brush. Glue dripped all over the newspapers on the table.

After a couple of tries, she started to improve. Olivia saw how much fun Marie was having. This made Olivia **happy**!

step 3

"Cover the bottom with pretty paper."

"How about I hand the papers to Marie and she can put them on the balloon?" Olivia suggested.

"That sounds like a GREAT idea!"
said Lucy.

GLUE

Together the sisters finished decorating the balloon bowl. Darcy even came over with the hairdryer to help the glue dry more quickly.

When the glue was finally dry, Lucy carefully popped the balloon.

"Wow! Look at what we can do when we all work together," said Lucy admiring the bowl they made.

"We have a great time when the first step is to **think of each other first!**"

THINK & TALK
ABOUT IT

Discuss the story...

1. Because the craft was difficult, what did Lucy say they would have to do?

2. What did Olivia do that was selfish? Why did she do that?

3. What did Lucy teach Olivia about being considerate?

4. After Olivia let Marie try to paint the glue on the balloon, what made Olivia happy?

5. What idea did Olivia have that helped them work together?

Discuss how to apply the story...

1. Can you think of a time when you had to work with other people to get something done?

2. Was it hard to work with other people?

3. Did you like working together?

4. How do you think working together can help get something done?

5. Next time, when you are playing a game or working on a craft with others, what is a way you can be considerate?

FOR PARENTS & MENTORS: *Help your child overcome selfishness by encouraging cooperative play. Cooperative play is when everyone works together to achieve a common goal. This type of play naturally encourages social growth and sharing. It helps children to not base their personal worth on winning or losing, but allows children to try new ideas while interacting with others and expressing their thoughts.*

LeBron's Festival gift

Today was the day for the Foster Care Kids Annual Festival. LeBron was so excited!

The Miller family often had kids from foster care stay with them for a while. LeBron loved playing with these kids and making new friends.

"Hey kids, this year we get to run the Bullseye Blitz game. This is a chance for us to serve other kids.

Please be on your best behavior and **think of the other kids first**," said Mr. Miller, LeBron's dad.

LeBron helped set up their booth.

He also looked at all the other games. There were so many *interesting* prizes and things to do!

44

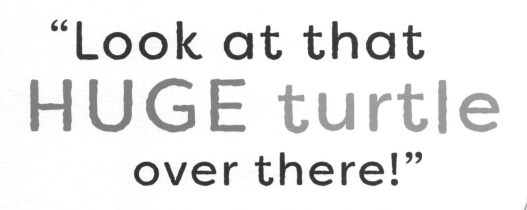

"Look at that HUGE turtle over there!"

Lucas said to LeBron.

"Whoa!" said LeBron looking at the giant stuffed turtle. "*Could you imagine* if Speedy ever got that big?" LeBron thought about their pet turtle at home.

LeBron and Lucas laughed as they pretended to be giant slow moving turtles.

"All right boys! It looks like kids are arriving," said their mom. LeBron enjoyed helping run the game. His older siblings, John and Emily, helped explain how to play the game to each new kid.

Getting into a rhythm, LeBron would pick
up the balls and Lucas would reset the game.

Sometimes a lot of kids were at their booth.

Other times no one was there.

During the slow times, their dad would take them to play the other games.

LeBron *hurried* over to the booth with the **cool** turtle prize. He had to throw the rings to loop around the floating ducks.

LeBron WON!

"His name will be Speedy Junior!" LeBron told his dad.

He went back to their booth
and *excitedly* told
Lucas all about it.

The festival was just about to end when one last little boy came up to their booth. The little boy *tried* and **tried**, but he was not able to win.

"Come on Billy! It is time to go," said his foster mom. Billy walked away with his head down. He was sad he could not win a prize.

LeBron saw how disappointed the boy was as he walked away. He looked at Speedy Junior. He grabbed the turtle and tried to catch the little boy before he left.

"I wanted you to have this. I saw how much you wanted a prize," LeBron said. "I already have a real turtle at home, so you can have this one. His name is Speedy Junior."

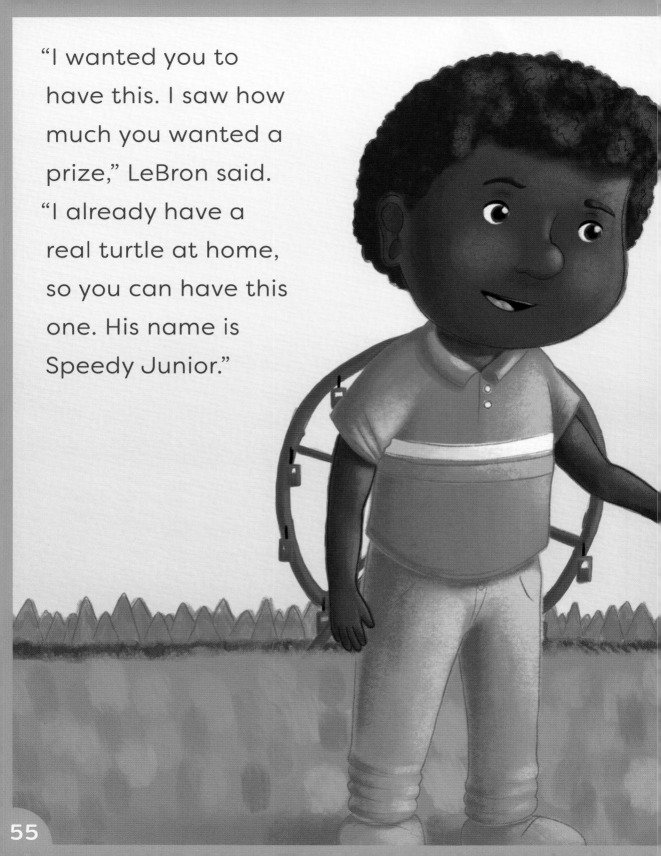

Billy's eyes got wide when LeBron handed him the turtle. He gave the turtle a big hug. "Thank you!" said the little boy.

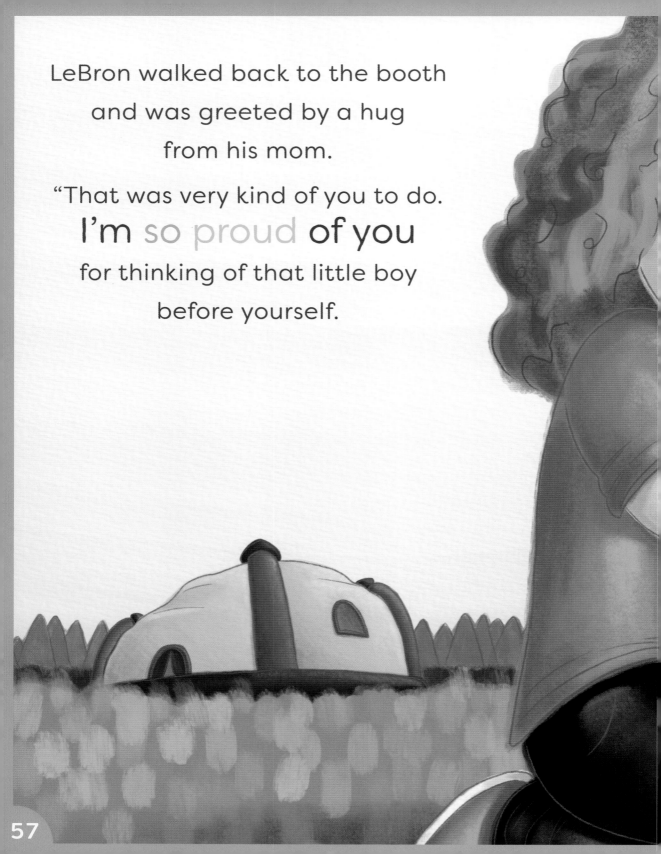

LeBron walked back to the booth
and was greeted by a hug
from his mom.

"That was very kind of you to do.
I'm so proud **of you**
for thinking of that little boy
before yourself.

LeBron helped his family
clean up the booth.
It made LeBron feel good
to know that he made
another boy happy.

THINK & TALK ABOUT IT

Discuss the story...

1. Why was LeBron's family going to the festival?

2. What did LeBron's dad ask LeBron and Lucas to do?

3. What are two ways LeBron helped with the game at the festival?

4. Why was the little boy sad?

5. How was LeBron considerate of others?

Discuss how to apply the story...

1. Have you ever given a gift to someone else?

2. How did that make you feel?

3. Has someone ever given you a special gift?

4. How did that make you feel?

5. What is something you can do to be considerate of others this week?

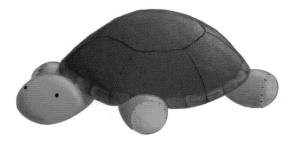

FOR PARENTS & MENTORS: *Children learn many behaviors, both good and bad, from their parents. If your kid sees you being considerate they are more likely to imitate that behavior. When you see a child being considerate toward others be sure to give them praise. Positive reinforcement is a great way to lock in good behavior.*

Meet the

mvpkids®

featured in
Stomp Out Selfishness™
with their families

YONG CHEN

LILLY CHEN
Sister

MR. JUN WANG
"Gong-Gong"
Grandfather

OLIVIA WAGNER

LUCY WAGNER TORRES
Sister

MARIE WAGNER
Sister

DARCY WAGNER
Sister

LeBRON MILLER

LUCAS MILLER

MRS. ELIZABETH MILLER
"Mom"

MR. JAMES MILLER
"Dad"

JOHN MILLER
Brother

EMILY MILLER
Sister

YONG CHEN

LEO RUSSO

FRANKIE RUSSO

JULIA ROJAS

GABBY GONZALEZ

AANYA PATEL

ANNIE JAMES

BLAKE JAMES

SARA COHEN-GOLDSTEIN